AMY PRAISES GOD IN POETRY

AMY FRANKLIN ANDREWS

Copyright © 2021 by **Amy Franklin Andrews**

All rights reserved. No part of this publication may be reproduced, distributed or transmitted in any form or by any means, including photocopying, recording, or other electronic or mechanical methods, without the prior written permission of the publisher, except in the case of brief quotations embodied in critical reviews and certain other noncommercial uses permitted by copyright law. For permission requests, write to the publisher, addressed "Attention: Permissions Coordinator," at the address below.

Amy Franklin Andrews/Rejoice Essential Publishing

PO BOX 512

Effingham, SC 29541

www.republishing.org

Unless otherwise indicated, scripture is taken from the King James Version.'

Scripture taken from the New King James Version®. Copyright © 1982 by Thomas Nelson. Used by permission. All rights reserved.

Amy Praises God In Poetry/Amy Franklin Andrews

ISBN-13: 978-1-952312-70-0
Library of Congress Control Number: 2021907170

MASTERS LIGHTS IN HIS DAUGHTERS HANDS

Dedication

*T*HIS BOOK IS DEDICATED to the Father God, who has been everything to me in this life. He keeps on sending wonderful godly men and women to encourage me to press on in His kingdom. Thank you to my parents, coach James Dean Franklin and Kate franklin. They saw the gifts in me at a young age and suggested that I continue to write. They also thought I would write enough poems for a book. Well, they were right. I also dedicate this book to Eddie and James Sharpe, my two boys who pushed me to be all I can for the Body of Christ and ultimately for myself. Thank you guys.

TABLE OF CONTENTS

ACKNOWLEDGMENT..ix

POEM 1:   Facing God's Mercy......................1

POEM 2:   His Seeds Of Blessings................4

POEM 3:   Ask Life..6

POEM 4:   Fiery Oven Of Anger
            And Hate..8

POEM 5:   From Evil Unto His
            Blessings......................................12

POEM 6:   A Life Of Praise..........................14

POEM 7:   Arrows Of The Enemy...............17

POEM 8:   The King's Strength And
            Power Forever And Ever...........20

POEM 9:   Make Ready For Life..................25

POEM 10:   A Countenance That Exalts

                    The Lord...................................27

POEM 11:   Heart's Desire............................30

POEM 12:   Given Up To Salvation...............33

POEM 13:   Destroy The Enemy...................36

POEM 14:   From The King's Lips................40

POEM 15:   Rejoicing In Salvation...............44

POEM 16:   Shall Not Be Moved...................47

ABOUT THE AUTHOR...51

Acknowledgment

I ALSO APPRECIATE MY FAMILY, who was always there to show me love so I could be free enough to go beyond my dreams in writing. To Regina and Terry Hill, Dani and Josh Street, Layla and Ashon, Terry Jr., Kera, Calob Hill, Lydia Brooks, Demonicia, Demonique, Edwin and Kim Franklin, Reginald, Angel and Angelicia Franklin, and Shannon Sharpe. I appreciate you all.

POEM 1

FACING GOD'S MERCY

*Y*OU HAVE ALL THAT word in your mouth and still, you let your walk go south.

You have so much knowledge in your heart.

Don't let anything pull you from God.

A mouth should praise and live in His truths.

Yet you still enjoy walking in negative fruits.

You have an opportunity to serve a living God.

Yet you turn away from our Savior, our Lord.

You know the truth because you've seen God move.

Hanging around the enemy's camp, you're destined to lose.

You've bowed before the King of King and praised His Holy Name.

There are no excuses because your knowledge makes them lame.

You have worshipped God and danced with the saints.

Give up your hopes for heaven because making it in, you ain't.

You've turned so far from the presence of God while sin grows wild and rampant in your heart.

God is a deliver. He has come to set us free.

All you have to do is repent and fall on your knees.

You let life's situations send you to hell without using the word that you know so well.

You can turn back to God and try to save yourself.

The love from Jesus will save you the same as everyone else.

Only God can clean your temple, that unclean house.

Your first love is wanting you to come on home. Then you won't have to fight all the battles alone.

God will perform a good work in you.

Let hate and evil go. You know what to do.

You can't deny that God was in your life.

Go ahead and let God back in. He will make it right.

Don't hold your head down. We've all fell short.

Get it right. Come on and give us a good report.

You are fearfully and wonderfully made.

We must trust in God and don't ever cave.

May the prayers of the righteous lead you to God's truth.

As you obey the call, humble yourself and do the Jesus in you.

You have all that word in your mouth and still, let your walk go south.

POEM 2

HIS SEEDS OF BLESSINGS

It's your time to get it done, for God has chosen you to be the powerful one.

Keep your head on straight and stay in your lane. Encourage yourself and don't complain.

Always stay ready and don't take down. Don't let fear turn you around.

Now it's your time to stand tall. Keep on praying or you are headed for a fall.

You can do it because the Lord is there. He will lead and guide you anywhere.

Fight, don't let your mind cause you fear. Be powerful. Don't get weary. Be strong my dear.

Don't you worry or don't you fret, for God Almighty, He ain't through with you yet.

Go forward for His power living in you. When the time comes, you'll know what to do.

God will show you how to walk and what to say. He will lead you, so forget all dismay.

God will take you through that straight and narrow path. Don't worry. He has never failed. Look at the power He has.

He is there whether you are sad or alone. God will never leave or forsake you.

So go ahead. Stay the course to get the job done. God has given you the power through Jesus Christ, His Son.

So lift us your hands, and endure to the end because with the Father, Son, and Holy Ghost, you are destined to win.

POEM 3

ASK LIFE

WHERE HAVE YOU BEEN? Where are you going? Where are you?
What did you say? What are you doing? What did you do?

What are you doing? What are you thinking? What do you need? What are you talking about?

Why did you say that? Why did you do that? Did you get that? Why are you doing that?

Why did you say that? Why do you think that? Why are you in it?

Who told you to get in it? Who told you to do it? Who told you to say it?

Who told you to think it? Who told you to believe it?

Who did it? Who told you to do it? Who did you do it to?

When did you get it? When did you do it? When did you go there?

When did you want to go there? When did you think it? When did you say it?

Be sure to know where, what, why, who, and when about the decisions that you make.

Because to know or not to know could be your life, for goodness sake.

Don't just do it because you feel it in your heart. You must be led by the Spirit of God.

POEM 4

FIERY OVEN OF ANGER AND HATE

ARE YOU OFFENDED THAT one can stand in the sun for hours and their skin color shows no difference, but another person can stand in the sun for the same amount of time and their skin becomes many shades?

Are you offended that one person's hair can swing loosely from the side without any natural body? They have such beautiful colors of blonde, red, and sandy hair. Another person's hair stands with body in its natural state which is mostly black in color.

FIERY OVEN OF ANGER AND HATE

Are you offended by the many skin colors of that one ethnicity while other races have only one or two shades? Are you offended by the figures of this race who are more pleasing than others?

Are you offended that some may have more than you while you have less than or nothing all? Are you offended knowing some people have better opportunities than some people ever will?

Are you offended that some people stick closer than others while others are holding knives to stab them in the back?

Are you offended that some are down cast and seem to have a harder time getting ahead while others seems to move right on ahead with no problem at all?

Yet is there no offense that the worms are in the ground and the squirrels in the trees? Is there no offense that the dog chases the cat or the trees and flowers give us breath?

Is there no offense that the rain and thunder come from the sky or the rivers flow in all directions as the sleet falls down in heavenlies? Is there no offense that mountains are so beautiful and the animals that live on them can be so dangerous?

Is there no offense that the land you walk on has springs of water underneath, yet we still walk on the ground? Or that the wind blows oh so gently through the leaves of a tree yet in a little they are turned another color and fall to the ground?

Is there no offense that the turtles crawl so show, yet the horses run so fast? Is there no offense that the sun shines so bright yet disappears over the horizon?

Did I create you or did you create me? We do not have the power to create such beauty, such ugliness, good, and bad,

We are offended at things in which we have no right, for we have created nothing. Then where does this offense come from?

You question things that you know not of. You did not create them. You are out of order therefore, you have no right to complain.

Who has given you the right to complain about someone else's works, works that you understand not?

Open your eyes and see the complete picture for these are the works of the Most High God, Father God, Jesus Christ, The Omnipotent One, I AM THAT I AM.

FIERY OVEN OF ANGER AND HATE

These works are great and stand alone. They are the works of a God of Power, a God of Love, a God for Life, a God of His Word, a God of Truth, a God of Salvation through His Son Jesus Christ who shed His Blood for all His people. THERE IS NO OFFENSE.

Everything was created in the image of our God. The trees, sun, rivers, sleet, birds, air, our bodies, our hair, our skin tones, and everything, He created all of it.

So if you find offense in the things our God has created, then you are not one of His and He knows you not. Now you be offended in this.

POEM 5

FROM EVIL UNTO HIS BLESSINGS

2ND CHRONICLES CHAPTER 7--VERSE 14

My sons and daughters, who are chosen by my identity, prefer my voice. Follow Christ's character and consider His lowliness. Speak your heart, bow down and cry out to me. Fold or bend your ways and reach up high above. Look to me and change. Find me and leave evil. Hunt me down and run from the wicked.

Fall on your face and stop your ridiculous conduct. Run to me and leave the devil behind.

Then I will stop being angry, forget your wrong doing, and not resent you for your mistakes.

I will not be taken back because of your short comings, or be upset because of your hiccups.

Then I will listen closely to you and make your earth well. I will receive and make your surroundings whole. I will be aware and touch your dwelling places. I will get wind of, make your ground solid, and restore the areas of my glory back to you.

My presence will be returned unto you.

POEM 6

A LIFE OF PRAISE

WHEN WE LIFT OUR hands up to the sky, is this giving God the praise?

When we sing songs from up on high, is this giving God the praise?

When we jump, shout and run around, is this giving God the praise?

When we sit quietly without a sound, is this giving God the praise?

When we clap our hands and stomp our feet, is this lifting God up?

When we move our bodies to that Holy Ghost sound, is this lifting God up?

When we shed a tear or shout out loud, is this lifting God up?

If we hug each other in the middle of a crowd, is this lifting God up?

If we greet each other with a Holy kiss, is this giving God Glory?

Knowing that nobody has a dance like this, is this giving God the Glory?

How about bowing down on your knees? Is this giving God the Glory?

While calling out loud, "Lord, help me please," is this giving God the Glory?

Maybe the joy of the Lord with smiles all around, is this your true praise?

Working in the church with no complains or frowns, is this your true praise?

Riding down the street praising God in your car, is this your true praise?

Living a holy life, so the world will know whose you are, is this your true praise?

The Word says all was created by Him.

So we must learn to worship in God's spiritual realm.

Rather you're a worshiper, a musician, or a preacher, no matter the case bowing down to God in every area of your life will reflect your pure praise.

POEM 7

ARROWS OF THE ENEMY

I FEEL SO WEIGHED DOWN in this crazy world with uncertain realities all around me.

I got to shake it off, the pain. There's no gain while all hope seems to flee.

My life seems to be going in circles, squares even, but never straight.

Searching for a purpose to be while seeking who I am, that's my take.

Walking toward my destiny while finding my way and leaning on my own thoughts, that's what my heart does say.

As I hear the uneven heart beating upon my chest, beating because its alive and full of life at its best.

But needing a healing from the loneliness, brokenness, and pain while living in this world of heartbreak, trying not to be ashamed.

All this while headed toward my future, I know I must leave my past behind.

There is no direction for my life, but I must keep searching for a sign.

Even though I will not pack up or go home, I will not let myself die if I can help it.

I will fight my way to a happy place, where a Higher Power can accept it.

Must try harder in every situation to make this life work.

This is the only life that I've been given before I'm turned to dirt.

There comes a time that we must fight for our existence and now it is mine.

Fight for peace, fight for joy, fight for righteousness, for I see it's past the time.

For I can still hear the prayers of my granny crying out to the One, who created it all, made it all, and continued to keep it all.

Through Jesus, His Son, The Father God and all His power will help me fight and win this war.

One day I may be able to seek God's promises allowing me to soar.

Find a peace within myself that I can share with others.

This love from God to spread among the lost sisters and brothers.

POEM 8

THE KING'S STRENGTH AND POWER FOREVER AND EVER

JEREMIAH CHAPTER 9 VERSE 23- 24

You say you know all and that your mind is great.

Wanting us all to follow you and watch you create.

Walking around thinking you are the greatest story ever told.

Never in my life have I seen anyone so bold.

With you and all your knowledge, your evil is standing out.

So what's up with that? What's that all about?

You pat yourself on the back in your situation.

Thinking you're all that with no hesitation.

Always hinting you're the smartest person alive, the next thing you'll be saying is that you have arrived.

Believing you are smarter than Almighty God Himself.

With that pumped up attitude, you think you don't need anyone else.

You use your knowledge as a toy to control.

What did you do, sell your soul to the devil?

I don't have to listen. Education is king.

Just look at me and all the intelligence I bring.

Your muscles make you the best, you think, but I know that's a lie.

Look at you with your nose turned all the way up to the sky.

Looking down on everyone because you can move a truck.

Yes, we can see your strength and that's probably just plain luck.

You can pick it up, push it, or flip it if you want.

AMY PRAISES GOD IN POETRY

Saying I'm so strong, I can make you believe me if you don't.

I have all the power. I'm the greatest man to be.

This is my gift to all. Count off one, two, three.

So you got plenty of money and your bank account is swole; cash, bonds, houses, land, jewelry and plenty of gold.

You think you are all that and a bag of chips.

People all around you, but they're afraid to give you lip.

You can't trust them because you are the one to get jived.

Look at me and all the accomplishments that I have acquired.

Now you are thinking about the next thing you are going to buy.

With everything you have, I really don't know why.

You may be small in stature, but you make your money work.

You don't help anyone or care about those you've hurt.

You even try to buy people when it suits you the most.

Stop bragging about your money. Shut up and don't you boast.

You buy your way in, then you buy your way out.

You're proud of your evil life, but brother there is a cost.

Jesus gave His life so we can be free.

So we can live a life of who He created us to be.

We know that the gifts of God will add no sorrow.

Your obedience can shorten or lengthen your destiny for tomorrow.

Keep focused on Him, who gave you wonderful gifts.

Read the word and live it. God will lead you toward a shift.

You can use your wisdom to teach those that haven't had the chance for knowledge.

Because some may learn slower than you, but baby, don't you knock it.

To have the power to pick or pull with power and strength.

Try using it to uphold honor and defend.

Use all your money to help those who have none.

You help me. I help another. That's how the battle is won.

Now God can really use you for good in this life.

Take time out for prayer and try to get it right.

You can't be walking around with a messed up attitude.

Because no one can beat God with the stuff He uses.

Live each day to glorify our awesome powerful God.

You are welcome into the Body of Christ, where a new life you can start.

POEM 9

MAKE READY FOR LIFE

LIFE AS WE KNOW it is no longer the same. Life as we know it has come to a change.

Life as we know it is not so stable. Life as we know it can sit us at the Master's table.

Life as we know it is so full of trials and pain. Life as we know it can give us everything.

Life as we know it can be full of tests. Life as we know it will let God have the mess.

Life as we know it can give us life and peace. Life as we know it will give us dreams to reach.

Life as we know it can change without notice. Life as we know it is like a book. I wonder who wrote it.

AMY PRAISES GOD IN POETRY

Life as we know it is not that fair. Life as we know it can have blessings everywhere.

Life as we know it can sometimes be rough. Life as we know it lets the word make us tough.

Life as we know it can loose us many things. Life as we know it brings many tears.

Life as we know it can take us to new levels. Life as we know it can push us to stomp the devil.

Life as we know it can lead us to God's truths. Life as we know it will clean the sin out of you.

Life as we know it will lead us to the Lord. Life as we know it lets gifts flow from your heart.

Life as we know it can be full of death. Life as we know it can fill us with wealth.

Life as we know it as we seek deep within. Life as we know it will let the Jesus in us win.

Life as we know it can help us overcome. Life as we know it, soon the final bell will be rung.

Life as we know it, we tried to live our best. Life as we know it will let God do the rest.

Life as we know it from since the baby you were born. Life as we know it praying to hear God's

Words, "well done."

POEM 10

A COUNTENANCE THAT EXALTS THE LORD

COME ON SISTERS OF the Most High God, as we walk this walk, we will do our part.

Casting all cares to Him because He cares for us. We will win because in God we trust.

Yes, we all have spiritual problems, but the prophets taught us that Jesus would solve them.

Don't judge others. Just look at yourself. Every one of us can use godly help.

Ministers, go ahead and praise with your feet and hands. With all those devils attacking, do all you can to stand.

Keep on preaching and cast those spirits out too. Come on Saints, for they will cast them out of you.

We're a fired up bunch of women and I'm not going to boast. Go ahead and preach the Father, Son, and Holy Ghost.

I thank God for the prophet teaching us the Word because it's the greatest most powerful thing I've ever heard and believed.

She binds up the devil and preaches the Hell out of us. Fighting the good fight can sometimes be tough.

They preach about faith, taking us to a place. If we stand fast in the Word, we'll see God's amazing grace.

Pressing us into a position for us to believe, so one day we will reign with God in the heavenlies.

The Holy Ghost is moving to bless us in this house. God is using the women of God and that is without a doubt.

It's a blessing to be a part of the worship and the praise, as God allows His Glory to fill this Holy place.

A COUNTENANCE THAT EXALTS THE LORD

So come on prophets your eyes lifted to the hills, let the spirit of God's word come while our souls be filled.

Minister that word. Set our hearts on fire. God will deliver. Our hands lifted to the sky.

The word is burning in your belly, wanting to come out. Preach that word prophet from the North, West, East, and South.

You teach us to forgive and come out of our mess, to humble ourselves so we can be blessed.

As we walk out those doors elevated in Him, in unity God will take us to a heavenly realm.

Men and women of God keep loving, preaching, teaching, and encouraging us to count it all joy as we stay focused and keep on reaching.

For the mark of the prize of the high calling in God pushes us to grow to walk in the ministry that's in our heart, to go out in the field to sow.

The anointing that you poured into our lives will grow larger than a mustard seed.

The only thing we have to do is pray to God and believe.

We praise God for your willingness to open your heart so deep.

Spirit of God continue to fall. Preacher and prophetess continue to preach.

POEM 11

HEART'S DESIRE

I love you Jesus, for you are my King of Kings.
   Wonderful and awesome, look at all the joy you bring.

You are loving and kind in all your ways.

You are my everything. You deserve my praise.

I glorify Your name in all I do.

I desire to be Holy just like you.

You breathed Your breath of life in me.

By your Holy Spirit, I do believe.

You are the truth and the way.

I bow before you every day.

You are the air, water, and sea.

I can sense your presence all over me.

HEART'S DESIRE

Lord, you are the wind, grass, and rain, a loving God that takes all my pain.

Father, You give me hope, joy, and peace.

In the middle of a struggle, it's You I seek.

I'm so thankful that You hear my prayer.

Giving all my trials to You because I know you care.

In the midst of turmoil, Lord, You stand tall.

You are even there for me whenever I fall.

As I come closer to You, I see more of myself.

What's so sad to say is that there is no one else to help.

With hands lifted up, I call unto thee.

I hunger for Your touch to comfort me.

Coming closer to You is my heart's desire.

I give you my life Lord. Hear my cry.

Lead and guide me from one realm to another.

Spirit of God dwell in me so I can help my sister and brother.

Let your glory fall in on this temple. Your anointing sets me free.

I pray your revelations from heaven down to me.

Your Word takes me deeper into your spiritual truths, but only for me if I keep praying unto you.

You speak words of encouragement continuously in my life, and pour your directions so I can keep on living right.

I seek your face while You fill my spirit man.

I speak your Holy anointed Word whenever I can.

You take total control and fill me with your presence.

Giving me a chance to love a God of many blessings.

Forgive me for my fleshy ways that take me away from you.

The precious Lamb of God that takes me straight to the truth.

Magnificent, merciful, powerful and absolute, omnipotent my God you are as we walk in your fruits.

Your glory fills me when I step in.

I bow to a God that has no sin, One who stands for all generations from beginning to the end.

Your promise to me is to be more than a friend, from everlasting to everlasting and ever more to be, to live and reign with You one day in eternity.

POEM 12

GIVEN UP TO SALVATION

God knows everything and every thought inside your head.

Leave those drugs alone and grab that Holy Word instead.

He will lead you out to a place of peace and joy.

Call upon His name and put the pistol down boy.

The Word will be your gun, knife, and that fist that you use so well.

You better listen bru I'm trying to keep you out of hell.

Give it up. Give it up. You can let Him take control.

Give your life to Jesus. He will surely save your soul.

He sent His Son, Jesus, to die upon the cross.
Giving us a chance to turn from our wicked ways and all.
You can be saved, delivered, and free from all that mess.
Turn your life around so God can bless, bless, and bless.
Give God a try and turn your life around.
Then you'll know for sure He's the best you've ever found.

Give it up. Give it up. You can let Him take control.
Give your life to Jesus. He will surely save your soul.

God has a path for you and you will never be alone.
We live in this world, but this is not our home.
You will become a blessing and bring others into Christ.

How does it feel now that you have a brand new life?

Now you will be able to give your testimony to all.

While walking in God doing the gifts in which you were called.

Give it up. Give it up. You can let Him take control.

Give your life to Jesus. He will surely save your soul.

POEM 13

DESTROY THE ENEMY

I'm tired of you devil. Get up out of my way.

I gave my life to God and now you want to play.

"No weapon formed against me shall prosper," saith the Lord.

You're not going to bind me anymore, trying to make my life hard.

I've come this far by faith and I will not turn back.

I will prosper, be in good health, and still will have no lack.

I'm on the right path now, so devil, you go ahead and depart.

Because when you try to come at me, I will call my Father, my Lord.

I will stand fast in the liberty of God because He has set me free.

Because baby, I'm not going to let that devil kill, steal, or destroy me.

I'm going to fight this good fight of faith. It's worth the fight.

God has been so good to me it makes me want to shout.

Fired up and ready to stomp that devil under my feet,

The way I move for God, Satan's got to loose those chains off me.

I take all God's authority that He has given to me.

I won't be tangled with the yokes of bondage that the devil tries to put on me.

Sit down devil somewhere and get up out of my face.

The God I serve won't allow you and Him to live up in this place.

I pray to the Lord that He will give me enough of His continued strength because devil you know the way you work don't make no kind of sense.

You had your time in the heavenlies with God but decided that wasn't enough.

But I'm got to keep on pressing toward the mark. You aren't going to mess me up.

Jesus gets all praises in my life because He brought me out.

I will serve the Lord forever in this temple, this house.

I'm going on with Jesus so devil loose me now.

I'm taking a stand in Jesus' name, so you might as well bow.

I thank God for His protection over my family and my life.

As I humble myself under His mighty hand, all will be made right.

Greater is He that's in me than him that's in the world.

You'll better stop playing around and come on with me girl.

I lift my hand up to you Lord, for you to take control.

Jesus will make a way out of no way and teach me to be bold.

He will lead and guide me and turn my life around.

He will deliver you and guide you by placing your feet on Holy Ground.

We grow up in Christ and learn the tricks of the enemy.

Watch out for some people around. They could just be frenemies sent straight from hell to drive you out of Him.

Just keep your eyes on Jesus. He will let you see their sins.

Stay away from those who's temples may be unclean, so the Spirit of God can heal our minds and bodies from everything.

Now I'm walking in God's Word because it is well and alive in me.

I'm sure the enemy is a little upset because I got the victory.

God is making me and getting rid of all the junk.

He's given me a chance to excel as He leavens out the lumps.

While I learn to completely submit and come closer to my Father, He teaching me to love others and become closer than a brother.

Now I live to please Him for all that He has done, and as I continue to stay rooted in Him the battle has been won.

POEM 14

FROM THE KING'S LIPS

I CAN DO ALL THINGS through Christ who strengthens me.

I am healed by His stripes, as you can see.

I am the head and not the tail, above and not beneath.

I'm blessed and favored by the Lord. I pray my soul He'll keep.

I'm blessed coming in and I'm blessed going out.

Life and death are in the power of the tongue. Life is pouring out my mouth.

This is the day that the Lord has made. God's mercy is new every morning.

Every day is a day of thanksgiving. For my Lord, I'll keep on running.

WORD, YOU GOT TO GET IT IN YOU.
WORD, YOU GOT TO LEARN TO WALK IT.
WORD, YOU GOT TO TELL ABOUT IT.
WORD, FROM THE KING'S LIPS.

If any of you lack wisdom, let him ask of God.

This body is the temple of the Holy Ghost and it belongs to the Lord.

I present myself to God as His living sacrifice.

I am more than a conquer through God's Son, Jesus Christ.

Goodness and mercy shall follow me all the days of my life.

I am strong in the Lord and in the power of His Might.

Thou I went through the fire, I shall not be burned.

What Satan meant for evil, God has already turned.

WORD, YOU GOT TO GET IT IN YOU.
WORD, YOU GOT TO LEARN TO WALK IT.

WORD, YOU GOT TO TELL ABOUT IT.
WORD, FROM THE KING'S LIPS.

God is my refuge and my fortress. My protection is here.

The Lord is the light of my salvation. Whom shall I fear?

Count it all joy when you fall into diverse temptations.

Trust in the Lord and do good. This is your foundation.

Humble yourself under God's Mighty hand and He will lift you up.

Many of the afflictions of the righteous, but our God will deliver us.

Seek the Lord while He may be found. Call Him while He is near.

He is the Lord that healeth us when there's no doubt or fear.

WORD, YOU GOT TO GET IT IN YOU.
WORD, YOU GOT TO LEARN TO WALK IT.

WORD, YOU GOT TO TELL ABOUT IT.
WORD, FROM THE KING'S LIPS.

So delight yourself in God and He'll give you the desires of your heart.

"My thoughts are not my thoughts nor your ways my ways," saith God.

Every good and perfect gift comes from the Father of lights.

Rejoice not in iniquity but rejoice in the truth that is right.

Create in me a clean heart and renew a right spirit in me.

Get wisdom and get understanding. Lord, we fear thee.

WORD, YOU GOT TO GET IT IN YOU.
WORD, YOU GOT TO LEARN TO WALK IT.

WORD, YOU GOT TO TELL ABOUT IT.
WORD, FROM THE KING'S LIPS.

POEM 15

REJOICING IN SALVATION

So you gave your life to God, now what are you going to do?

Find a church that can teach you about God's Word and truth.

Separate yourself from those friends that are still in sin, or maybe tell them what changed your life and helped to bring you in.

I know it may be hard to let some of them go.

God has saved you for a reason, so it's best to tell them no.

Come into the house of God expecting the best for your life.

The church is a place for all to heal and grow away from strife.

Now that you are saved, your true life has only just begun.

So read the Word and apply it. God will surely be your friend.

Make sure you find a good church because anything won't do.

There's a lot of devils in the church to hinder us.

Get yourself a prayer life and let Jesus do the work.

Some things we must let go of and yes, some things will hurt.

Prayer is a powerful tool used for the Body of Christ.

Just stay focus on Jesus. He will turn and change your life.

Sometimes we don't read the Word, but it has all God's directions.

As you learn of God's promises, then you'll learn of His affections.

The Word will heal your body and give you a brand new mind.

Learn the fruits of the spirit: love, joy, peace, patience, and kindness.

Put on the heavenly Word daily just like a pair of jeans.

It will bring you closer to our God and He will truly make you clean.

Salvation is a time for change in any season.

A time to press for a better life and that's an awesome reason.

We can grow to different levels if we surrender all to God, and let those hidden secret sins leave out of your heart.

For you will never have a greater opportunity in your life than this, to make that final role call and to make God's precious list.

POEM 16

SHALL NOT BE MOVED

Can't nobody stop me from what I'm about to do.

Because only Christ, our Savior, has a claim on me and you.

Thank God for a made up mind to stay in the Word.

When I read it, it sounds like music, the sweetest thing I've heard.

I had to push myself to get in it, so I could go to another level.

I have no time to play around with the same mean old devils.

I must go ahead and follow the course that God has for me.

I'm going all the way with Jesus. Just you wait and see.

THE WINDOWS OF HEAVEN ARE OPEN FOR YOU TO GET BLESSED, BLESSED, BLESSED.

YOU CAN'T LET NOBODY STOP YOU. YOU GOT TO JUST PRESS, PRESS, PRESS.

Praying a prayer to God to lead me on the way, believing in His miracles that bless me from day to day.

I'm standing on the Word that gives me strength and hope while He is teaching me to live like the true and sanctified folk.

I know He's got my back. I do all I can to obey.

Apply the Word daily and do exactly what it says.

Yes, He does chastise me. He has an overwhelming love.

His blessings are ever upon me sent by the Father of lights from above.

THE WINDOWS OF HEAVEN ARE OPEN FOR YOU TO GET BLESSED, BLESSED, BLESSED.

YOU CAN'T LET NOBODY STOP YOU. YOU GOT TO JUST PRESS, PRESS, PRESS.

I'm pressing in for my family. I'm pressing in for the Lord.

As I continue to seek His face, I have to do my part.

So many people are hurting. So many people are in grief.

The Word will help a lot of people turn over a brand new leaf.

I must keep on keeping on as He reveals His truth from within.

The more I walk in the Word, the more I'm destined to win.

I got to keep my eyes on Jesus, for He will continue to bring me through.

The closer you are to Jesus, He'll push troubles back from you.

THE WINDOWS OF HEAVEN ARE OPEN FOR YOU TO GET BLESSED, BLESSED, BLESSED,

YOU CAN'T LET NOBODY STOP YOU. YOU GOT TO JUST PRESS, PRESS, PRESS.

Now, remember God gets all the glory. That is something He doesn't share.

He will take you all over the world and use you everywhere.

You just have to learn it's all about Him and not you.

Laborers are needed in the field. Don't worry, there is plenty of work to do.

We must press our way through trials while our eyes are looking up to heaven above and watch our Lord and Savior take us to a higher place of love.

THE WINDOWS OF HEAVEN ARE OPEN FOR YOU TO GET BLESSED, BLESSED, BLESSED.

YOU CAN'T LET ANYBODY STOP YOU. YOU GOT TO JUST PRESS, PRESS, PRESS.

About The Author

AMY FRANKLIN ANDREWS HAS always had a passion for writing and singing. She would often stay up all night reading any book that she could find. In school, Amy Franklin Andrews won a writing contest. At that moment, she realized that writing was a gift from God. After graduating from Southern Union State Junior College, Amy Franklin Andrews continued to write poems at various places: on her jobs, church anniversaries, and programs where she was asked to read her poetry. "Amy Praises God In Poetry," has been a long time coming and glorifies God. Amy Andrews is ecstatic to see lives transformed as she operates in God's gifting on her life.

Index

A

accomplishments, 22
affections, 45
afflictions, 42
afraid, 22
alive, 17, 21, 39
Almighty, 4, 21
Amy Franklin Andrews, 51
angry, 13
animals, 9
anointing, 29, 31
ashamed, 18
attitude, 21, 24

B
baby, 23, 26, 37
bank account, 22
battle, 23, 39

battles, 2
beautiful, 8, 9
beauty, 10
believe, 6, 22, 28, 29, 30
blessings, 26, 32, 48
Blood, 11
boast, 23, 28
bodies, 11, 14, 39
Body of Christ, 24, 45
bold, 21, 38
bondage, 37
bonds, 22
bowed, 2
bragging, 23
brokenness, 18
brother, 23, 31, 39

C

camp, 1
cares, 27
cash, 22
Casting, 27
character, 12
chest, 17
Christ, 5, 10, 11, 12, 34, 39, 40, 41, 47

church, 15, 44, 45, 51
colors, 8, 9
comfort, 31
complain, 4, 10
complains, 15
conduct, 12
control, 21, 32, 33, 34, 35, 38
cross, 34
crowd, 15

D

danced, 2
dangerous, 9
daughters, 12
death, 26, 40
decisions, 7
deliver, 2, 29, 39, 42
delivered, 34
depart, 36
desires, 43
destined, 1, 5, 49
destiny, 17, 23
devil, 12, 21, 26, 28, 36, 37, 38
directions, 9, 32, 45
doors, 29

doubt, 28, 42
drugs, 33
dwelling, 13

E

earth, 13
Education, 21
Encourage, 4
encouragement, 32
endure, 5
enemy, 1, 39
enjoy, 1
ethnicity, 9
everlasting, 32
evil, 3, 12, 21, 23, 41
excel, 39
excuses, 2
existence, 18
eyes, 10, 29, 39, 49, 50

F

faith, 28, 36, 37
family, 38, 49
Father, 5, 10, 18, 28, 31, 37, 39, 43, 48

Index

favored, 40
fear, 4, 42, 43
fearfully, 3
feet, 14, 27, 37, 39
fight, 2, 18, 28, 37
fire, 29, 41
flowers, 9
forsake, 5
fortress, 42
foundation, 42
frenemies, 39
fret, 4
frowns, 15
fruits, 1, 32, 45
future, 18

G

gain, 17
generations, 32
gift, 22, 43, 51
girl, 38
glorify, 24, 30
glory, 13, 31, 32, 50
God, 1, 2, 3, 4, 5, 7, 10, 11, 14, 15, 16, 18, 19, 21, 23, 24, 25, 26, 27, 28, 29, 31, 32, 34, 35, 36, 37,

38, 39, 40, 41, 42, 43, 44, 45, 46, 47, 48, 50, 51, 52
gold, 22
Goodness, 41
grace, 28
grief, 49
ground, 9, 10, 13
guide, 4, 31, 38, 39

H

hair, 8, 11
hate, 3
health, 36
heart, 1, 2, 7, 12, 17, 26, 29, 31, 43, 46
hearts, 29
heaven, 2, 31, 50
heavenlies, 9, 28, 38
Hell, 28
help, 15, 18, 22, 23, 26, 27, 31, 49
hesitation, 21
hiccups, 13
hills, 29
Holy, 2, 5, 14, 15, 28, 30, 32, 33, 39, 41
home, 2, 18, 34
hope, 17, 31, 48

hopes, 2
horizon, 10
horses, 10
houses, 22
humble, 3, 29, 38
hurt, 22, 45

I

identity, 12
iniquity, 43
intelligence, 21

J

jeans, 45
Jesus, 2, 3, 5, 10, 11, 18, 23, 26, 27, 30, 34, 35, 38, 39, 41, 45, 48, 49
jewelry, 22
job, 5
joy, 15, 18, 29, 30, 31, 33, 42, 45
judge, 27
jump, 14

K

kindness, 45
King, 2, 30
knife, 33
knowledge, 1, 2, 21, 23

L

Laborers, 50
lame, 2
lane, 4
leaves, 10
liberty, 37
life, 2, 3, 7, 15, 16, 17, 18, 21, 23, 24, 25, 30, 31, 32, 34, 35, 36, 38, 41, 44, 45, 46, 52
Life, 11, 25, 26, 40
loneliness, 18
Lord, 1, 4, 15, 26, 31, 36, 37, 38, 40, 41, 42, 43, 49, 50
lose, 1
love, 2, 19, 30, 32, 39, 45, 48, 50
lumps, 39

M

mark, 29, 38
mercy, 40, 41

mind, 4, 20, 45, 47
Ministers, 27
ministry, 29
miracles, 48
mistakes, 13
money, 22, 23
Most High, 10, 27
mountains, 9
mouth, 1, 3, 40
muscles, 21
musician, 16
mustard seed, 29

N

nose, 21

O

obedience, 23
obey, 3, 48
offended, 8, 9, 10, 11
offense, 9, 10, 11
omnipotent, 32
Omnipotent, 10
opportunities, 9

opportunity, 1, 46
overcome, 26
overwhelming, 48

P

pain, 17, 18, 25, 31
path, 5, 34, 36
patience, 45
peace, 18, 19, 25, 31, 33, 45
picture, 10
pistol, 33
poetry, 51
power, 5, 10, 18, 22, 23, 40, 41
Power, 11, 18
powerful, 4, 24, 28, 32, 45
praise, 1, 14, 15, 16, 27, 28, 29, 30
praised, 2
praises, 38
prayers, 3, 18
praying, 4, 26, 31
preacher, 16
Preacher, 29
preaches, 28
preaching, 28, 29
presence, 2, 13, 30, 32

prize, 29
prophetess, 29
prophets, 27, 29
prosper, 36
protection, 38, 42
purpose, 17

Q

question, 10

R

race, 9
rain, 9, 31
realities, 17
refuge, 42
reign, 28, 32
Rejoice, 43
resent, 13
restore, 13
revelations, 31
righteous, 3, 42
righteousness, 18
rivers, 9, 11

S

saints, 2
Saints, 28
salvation, 42
Salvation, 11, 46
Satan, 37, 41
save, 2, 34, 35
Savior, 1, 47, 50
season, 46
secret, 46
sense, 30, 37
share, 19, 50
sin, 2, 26, 32, 44
sing, 14
singing., 51
situation, 18, 21
skin, 8, 9, 11
sky, 9, 14, 21, 29
smarter, 21
smiles, 15
soar, 18
Son, 5, 11, 18, 28, 34, 41
songs, 14
sons, 12
sorrow, 23

sound, 14
south, 1, 3
sow, 29
Spirit, 7, 29, 30, 31, 39
spiritual problems, 27
spiritual realm, 15
springs, 10
squirrels, 9
stab, 9
stature, 22
stomp, 14, 26, 37
story, 20
street, 15
strength, 21, 23, 37, 48
stripes, 40
strong, 4, 22, 41
submit, 39
suits, 22
sun, 8, 10, 11

T

tail, 40
tear, 15
temple, 2, 31, 38, 41
temples, 39

temptations, 42
testimony, 35
thanksgiving, 41
thinking, 6, 20, 22
thoughts, 17, 43
thunder, 9
tongue, 40
toy, 21
trees, 9, 11
trials, 25, 31, 50
troubles, 49
truck, 21
truth, 1, 3, 30, 32, 43, 44, 49
truths, 1, 26, 31
turmoil, 31
turtles, 10

U

ugliness, 10
unclean, 2, 39
understand, 10

V

victory, 39

Index

voice, 12

W

walk, 1, 3, 5, 10, 27, 29, 32, 49
Walking, 17, 20
weapon, 36
weary, 4
wicked, 12, 34
willingness, 29
win, 5, 18, 26, 27, 49
wind, 10, 13, 31
wisdom, 23, 41, 43
women, 28, 29
wonderfully, 3
Word, 11, 15, 28, 31, 32, 33, 39, 44, 45, 47, 48, 49
work, 2, 18, 22, 37, 45, 50
world, 15, 17, 18, 34, 38, 50
worms, 9
worry, 4, 5, 50
worship, 15, 28
worshiper, 16
worshippe

AMY PRAISES GOD IN POETRY

www.ingramcontent.com/pod-product-compliance
Lightning Source LLC
Chambersburg PA
CBHW052120110526
44592CB00013B/1690